Original title:
Through Brokenness

Copyright © 2024 Swan Charm
All rights reserved.

Author: Eliora Lumiste
ISBN HARDBACK: 978-9916-79-042-7
ISBN PAPERBACK: 978-9916-79-043-4
ISBN EBOOK: 978-9916-79-044-1

## From Shattered to Shimmering

In the quiet of despair, we stand,
Pieces scattered, like grains of sand.
Hope flickers faintly, a distant gleam,
But deep inside, we dare to dream.

Each shard a story, a tale untold,
Whispers of courage, both timid and bold.
We gather the fragments, mend with care,
With every heartbeat, we rise from despair.

The journey is tough, a winding road,
With moments of doubt, a heavy load.
Yet light breaks through, illuminating our way,
As we embrace the dawn of a new day.

From ashes of sorrow, we start to glow,
In the warmth of resilience, our spirits grow.
Each bruise we carry, an emblem of fight,
And together we shine, burning ever so bright.

So here's to the shattered, the radiant, the free,
Together we forge our own destiny.
With every step taken, we rise and transform,
From shattered to shimmering, we weather the storm.

## **Dancing Amidst the Fractures**

In shadows cast by broken glass,
We twirl and sway where others pass.
Each step a whisper, every glance,
A chance to find our fractured dance.

The ground beneath, a jagged floor,
Yet still we seek and search for more.
With every leap, we rise above,
Embracing scars, we learn to love.

**Finding Strength in the Shatter**

From shattered pieces, we ignite,
A fire born from darkest night.
With every crack, a story tells,
A seed of strength within us dwells.

Embracing pain, we rise anew,
In fractured light, the old feels true.
We mend the wounds with gentle care,
And find our strength, it's always there.

## Threads of Light in the Dark

In deepest dark, a beacon glows,
With threads of light, the courage grows.
We seek the stars above the haze,
Illuminating life's lost maze.

Through darkest nights, we find our way,
With every step, the dawn will play.
The beauty lies in fragile seams,
A tapestry of vibrant dreams.

## The Cradle of Broken Dreams

Within the cradle, dreams take flight,
Each one a flicker in the night.
Though some may fade and slip away,
New visions bloom with dawn's first ray.

In gentle hands, we hold the past,
And cherish moments that can't last.
For in this place of tender sighs,
Resilience finds us, as night dies.

# Healing in Cracks

In the walls where shadows seep,
Silent stories, secrets keep.
Cracks that whisper tales of old,
Of broken hearts and spirits bold.

Nature finds a way to mend,
In every fissure, life can blend.
Tiny roots and moss will grow,
In the broken, new life shows.

Sunlight dances on the scars,
Hope descends like shining stars.
Each imperfection tells a tale,
Of resilience where we prevail.

Through the cracks, our light breaks through,
Healing colors in shades of blue.
Each fracture holds a spark of grace,
A testament to time and space.

Though we bear our battle's mark,
From our wounds, we find a spark.
Healing blooms in every crack,
A journey forward, no turning back.

## The Beauty in Ashes

In the stillness after fire,
Memories dance in soft desire.
From the ruins, life can rise,
A phoenix born, a bright surprise.

Dust settles on forgotten dreams,
But in darkness, vibrant gleams.
The ashes cradle what once lived,
Each remnant, a lesson to give.

New beginnings in charred remains,
Life's cycle in its endless chains.
Beauty found in what decays,
Through the sorrow, hope still plays.

In the heart of every end,
Lies a chance to start again.
Sprouting seeds in smoky air,
A brighter path, we learn to care.

Embrace the scars of yesterday,
For in the ashes, dreams replay.
Resilient, we will rise and soar,
Finding beauty forevermore.

# **Fractals of Hope**

Patterns woven in life's design,
Each twist and turn, a sacred sign.
Fractals bloom in vibrant hues,
Reminding us of paths to choose.

In chaos, order finds its place,
Every fragment has its grace.
Infinite journeys, not confined,
Hope resides in what we find.

The echoes of our dreams unfold,
Like fractals, stories yet untold.
Dive deeper into every role,
Infinite beauty speaks to the soul.

With every setback, lessons bloom,
In the darkest night, hope finds room.
Each reflection, a guiding star,
Fractals remind us who we are.

In the vastness of the unknown,
Hope's Prism shines, brightly shown.
Together, let us weave and cope,
Life's fractals are threads of hope.

## **Rebirth from Splinters**

From broken wood, new life emerges,
A tapestry of strength surges.
Splinters sharp yet beauty found,
In these remnants, hope is crowned.

Nature teaches with gentle hands,
How to stand where sorrow stands.
In the fragments, stories blend,
Rebirth waits around each bend.

In the quiet, whispers bloom,
From the shards, dispelling gloom.
Each splinter tells of battles fought,
Of lessons deep and wisdom sought.

In the cracks, the sunlight plays,
Transforming shadows into rays.
What was lost, now intertwines,
A mosaic of life, it shines.

Through the pain, we learn to grow,
From every fissure, new seeds sow.
Rebirth from splinters, we shall rise,
The beauty found in our goodbyes.

## The Color of Broken Dreams

Whispers of hope fade to gray,
Echoes of laughter lost in the fray.
Shattered fragments on the floor,
Painting the heart, forever sore.

Shadows of wishes long gone by,
Silent prayers to the weary sky.
Each broken piece tells a tale,
Of faded glory, soft and pale.

In the dusk of forgotten night,
A glimmer of courage still ignites.
Among the ruins, a spark remains,
A flicker of joy in the strains.

Through the cracks flows a sweet refrain,
Lessons learned, love's gentle pain.
Though darkness clings, light will glean,
The beauty found in broken dreams.

## Dancing with the Fractures

Waltzing on the edge of fate,
Twists and turns, it's never late.
In the silence, rhythms beat,
Embracing wounds, a bittersweet.

Each scar a step, a silent song,
Through shattered moments, we belong.
With every fracture, joy is spun,
Dancing till the night is done.

Footprints etched in whispered sighs,
Tracking paths beneath dark skies.
With each stumble, we find grace,
In this dance, we find our place.

Harmony found in broken parts,
A symphony of healing hearts.
Together we sway, despite the pain,
In the chaos, love will reign.

So let us twirl through shadows cast,
For in this dance, we're free at last.
With every heartbeat, fear will fade,
In the embrace of wounds displayed.

## Etchings of Survival

Stories carved in fragile skin,
Resilience lies where scars begin.
Each line a testament, a fight,
In the dark, we search for light.

With battle wounds that never fade,
Echoes of strength, unafraid.
In silence, courage speaks so loud,
We rise again, fiercely proud.

The weight of sorrow, a heavy cloak,
Yet from the ashes, we will soak.
Fingers trace the lines of fate,
In every breath, we celebrate.

Moments pause, then surge like tides,
Through the chaos, hope abides.
Etched in time, our spirits soar,
With every trial, we are more.

Embrace the scars, they tell the tale,
Of journeys taken, hearts that prevail.
In the tapestry of what we've braved,
Etchings of survival, forever saved.

**A Tapestry of Wounds**

Threads of sorrow, colors bright,
Weaving pain into the night.
Every stitch a story told,
A tapestry of dreams unrolled.

In the fibers, strength entwined,
Binding memories of the mind.
Soft reminders of battles fought,
In each detail, life is caught.

Through the frays and gentle tears,
We find solace through the years.
In the fabric's warm embrace,
Lies the mark of every place.

Stitched with love and tender care,
A reminder that we're always there.
Through the bruises and the bends,
A tapestry that never ends.

Embodying the scars we wear,
Life's rich journey, a tale to share.
In the weavings, hope is found,
A tapestry of wounds profound.

**Unraveled Threads**

In shadows cast by fading light,
Frayed edges whisper tales of night.
Each knot undone reveals the wear,
A tapestry of dreams laid bare.

Beneath the weight of woven pain,
We find our strength, we break the chain.
Amid the strands that come apart,
New patterns form, a fresh start.

The threads entwined, a colorful maze,
Breathe life anew with vibrant gaze.
Through tangled paths, we dance and weave,
Reclaiming hope that we believe.

As old seams stretch, we learn to grow,
To hurt and heal in ebb and flow.
Each unraveling, a brand-new face,
In time's embrace, we find our place.

So let the threads unfurl with grace,
In the unknown, we find our space.
For every twist, a lesson clear,
In the unraveling, we draw near.

## **Tenderness in the Tattered**

Within the rips of weathered cloth,
Lie stories sung, both soft and wroth.
The edges worn, a gentle sigh,
Hold warmth enough for days gone by.

In folds that speak of love's embrace,
There lies a truth, a sacred place.
Even when tattered, hearts can mend,
Through every loss, we learn to bend.

So lift the fray, and in the tears,
Find solace sweet and shed your fears.
For tenderness in worn-out seams,
Can stitch us whole, revive our dreams.

Each faded thread, a memory keeps,
Reminds us of the love that weeps.
In tattered garments, warmth is found,
In fragile threads, we stand our ground.

Though time may pull, and life may fray,
We wear our scars, come what may.
With tender hearts, we face the night,
In tattered beauty, we find light.

## Navigating the Shards

Amidst the fragments, sharp and still,
We move with caution, against the chill.
Each shattered piece, a tale to tell,
In navigating wounds, we learn so well.

With every cut, a lesson learned,
In broken paths, new fires burned.
The shards may glisten, lure our gaze,
Yet strength grows deeper through the maze.

We step with care, but hearts ablaze,
Transforming pain into a praise.
From chaos birthed, our courage glows,
In tender moments, resilience flows.

As light refracts through fractured glass,
We see our past but choose to pass.
For journeying through the sharpest turns,
In navigating shards, our spirit yearns.

Boundless, we rise from every fall,
With every step, we answer the call.
Through all the cuts, our strength expands,
Embracing shards with willing hands.

## **Unearthing Strength from Strain**

Beneath the weight of worn-out days,
We seek the light in tangled ways.
Through burdens thick, we start to see,
The roots of strength that set us free.

In trials faced, we find our ground,
In every struggle, growth is found.
For strain unveils a hidden force,
Guiding us gently on our course.

With every tear, a seed is sown,
In weary hearts, new hope is grown.
Amidst the chaos, love will blaze,
Unearthing strength within the maze.

So let us stand, though weary bones,
Through every ache, we claim our own.
For strain, though heavy, clears the way,
To find the strength in disarray.

As burdens shift and shadows fade,
We rise anew, unafraid.
In every challenge, let us train,
To unearth strength from all the strain.

## **Fissures of Understanding**

In shadows deep, we seek the light,
Where thoughts collide in silent fight.
A whisper here, a heartbeat's pause,
We stitch our wounds with gentle laws.

Across the void, our voices strain,
Each word a drop of joy or pain.
With open minds, we start to trace,
The fragile lines of our embrace.

In every crack, a story waits,
To mend the bond that time negates.
With every word, a seed is sown,
In fissures deep, we find our own.

So as we walk this winding road,
Through doubts and fears, we share the load.
In understanding, love will grow,
And heal the fissures that we show.

Together, let's weave a tapestry,
Of thoughts and dreams in harmony.
For in this dance of give and take,
We find the truth that will not break.

## Born from the Shards

From broken glass, we rise anew,
In every shard, a different view.
We shape our dreams from fractured bits,
With courage born from painful hits.

Each jagged edge, a lesson teaches,
In silent nights, the heart still reaches.
Through storms we've weathered, hearts laid bare,
We craft our paths with tender care.

From ashes grey, the phoenix flies,
A testament to all our tries.
With spirit fierce and voices loud,
We stand together, hearts unbowed.

In every scar, a story grows,
A mark of where the struggle flows.
So let us sing, embrace the parts,
From broken dreams, we build our hearts.

For in each fissure, beauty shines,
In every tear, a thread aligns.
From darkness deep, and pain we've known,
Born from the shards, we find our throne.

# Songs of the Undaunted

In the face of fear, we raise our song,
With echoes strong, we march along.
Through trials thick, our voices rise,
With hope aglow in stormy skies.

Together we stand, shoulder to shoulder,
In unity, we grow bolder.
With every note, our spirits soar,
A symphony of hearts that roar.

For every tear that's ever shed,
We turn to strength, not dread.
With rhythm found in every beat,
Our anthem calls, we won't retreat.

In shadows cast by doubt and fear,
We fight as one, our purpose clear.
For every dream that's lost or found,
We sing our truth, profound, unbound.

Embracing life, the highs, the lows,
Each battle fought, our courage grows.
In every song, we find our way,
The undaunted hearts will always stay.

# Embracing the Fray

In chaos wild, our spirits dance,
We face the storm, we take the chance.
Through every clash, our voices blend,
With every step, we will defend.

As waves crash hard against the shore,
We stand our ground, we seek for more.
In turmoil's heart, we find our grace,
Embracing all, we take our place.

With open arms, we greet the night,
In shadows deep, we find our light.
Through trials fierce and tempests wild,
We see the world through eyes of a child.

For in the fray, our souls ignite,
With every struggle, we take flight.
Through pain and doubt, we move as one,
In unity, we've just begun.

So here we stand, unbowed, unbroken,
With words of truth, our hearts are spoken.
In every fight, our courage stays,
Together, we embrace the fray.

## Healing in Fragments

In shards of light, a story grows,
Where broken pieces start to glow.
Time weaves gently through the seams,
Mending what once broke at the seams.

Each tear a thread, each scar a line,
In this tapestry, I find what's mine.
The heart, though cracked, beats true and bold,
In the warmth of love, the spirit's gold.

I gather fragments, one by one,
With every sunrise, a new begun.
Hope whispers softly, 'You are whole',
In every crack, there's room for soul.

With patience, light begins to seep,
Into the shadows, where sorrows creep.
Through the journey, pain transforms,
Into the beauty that love warms.

In fragments healed, I learn to see,
Life's intricate art, wild and free.
Embracing flaws, I find my way,
In healing's dance, I dare to stay.

## The Beauty of Wounded Wings

Wounded wings that dare to fly,
Paint the canvas of the sky.
Each scar a tale of battles fought,
In silent grace, redemption sought.

The broken beauty sings aloud,
In every heart, a brave avowed.
Fragile strength in the face of pain,
A vibrant song, a silver rain.

Through the storms, they learn to soar,
The more they bleed, the more they roar.
Every hushed whisper, a call to rise,
In unexpected ways, life's surprise.

In twilight's glow, wings shimmer bright,
Once darkened paths now painted light.
A journey woven with threads of grace,
Through wounds we find a sacred place.

In the hush of night, they find their song,
With every note, they grow more strong.
The beauty of the wounded flight,
Turns darkest sorrow into light.

## Mosaic of Pain

Shattered pieces on the floor,
Each one tells what I endure.
In colors deep, the pain is cast,
A beautiful chaos from the past.

Every sharp edge holds a tale,
Of how I stumbled, how I failed.
Yet in the mess, a work of art,
A broken heart can still impart.

With careful hands, I glue each part,
Creating beauty from the heart.
In quiet moments, the truth breaks through,
In every flaw, there's strength anew.

Layers thick with history's weight,
Crafting resilience from heartbreak's fate.
A vibrant mosaic, flawed yet bright,
In pain's embrace, I find my light.

As pieces join, a vision blooms,
In the fragments, love resumes.
Through pain's lens, I learn to see,
A masterpiece, just waiting to be.

## Fragments of Hope

In the quiet dawn, whispers rise,
Little fragments fill the skies.
Each twinkling star, a gleam of fate,
In these pieces, we contemplate.

Torn pages hold a story's start,
With every end, a fresh new part.
The past may linger, shadows dance,
But hope ignites a brave new chance.

With every trial, a lesson learned,
Through ashes gray, a fire burned.
In shattered dreams, a spark we find,
Fragments of hope that bind mankind.

We gather bits, like scattered grains,
In every struggle, love remains.
Through autumn's chill or winter's glare,
Hope's gentle breath fills the air.

As seasons shift, we learn and grow,
In every heart, the light will show.
Embrace the shards, let the light in,
In fragments of hope, new beginnings begin.

## **Lighthouses in the Dark**

In shadows deep, a beacon shines,
A guiding light through stormy times.
With every wave, its courage stands,
A whisper sweet from distant lands.

Through thunder's roar, through howling winds,
It calls to souls, where hope begins.
A steadfast watch, through nights so long,
Where broken dreams can still be strong.

The lighthouse beams on rocky shores,
Its light a promise, forever pours.
Navigators lost, their hearts awry,
Find solace in the trembling sky.

The keeper's heart, like flame, will burn,
For every ship, a safe return.
In darkest nights, its power glows,
A tale of strength that never slows.

So cherish those who stand so tall,
In life's tempest, they guide us all.
With every flash, a spark of grace,
We'll find our path, in this vast space.

## Journeys through the Fractured

We walk upon these broken roads,
With every step, a heavy load.
But through the cracks, the light can seep,
A promise made, our souls to keep.

In shattered dreams, we learn to breathe,
Through fractured paths, we start to weave.
Each journey carved with lessons true,
In pieces found, we are renewed.

The cracks become our strength and guide,
In every fault, we do not hide.
For through the pain, we see a chance,
To rise again, and learn to dance.

Through storms we rise, through trials faced,
With every wound, our hearts embraced.
In every fall, a chance to grow,
Through fractured ways, our spirits glow.

We cherish scars, the stories told,
In every step, the brave and bold.
For journeys marked in cracks and pain,
Can lead us home, through joy and rain.

## **Depths of Resilience**

In quiet depths, where shadows play,
A spark ignites, to light the way.
Through storms we face, and trials bend,
The heart holds strong, as battles end.

Like roots that dig through hardened ground,
In silence, strength is often found.
We rise again, despite the scars,
Our spirits shine like distant stars.

Each challenge bold, we face anew,
In every loss, a strength so true.
Through depths explored, our minds expand,
The spirit's will, a guiding hand.

With every fall, we learn to rise,
In shattered dreams, the dawn will prize.
The depths of life, both dark and bright,
Transform our souls, ignite the fight.

Through deep blue seas and skies of gray,
Resilience blooms, come what may.
In every wave, we stand our ground,
In depths of strength, we're glory-bound.

## Recovering the Mosaic

In shattered pieces, beauty lies,
A mosaic formed through tear-streaked eyes.
Each fragment tells a tale of pain,
Yet woven close, a strength remains.

With every shard, we craft anew,
A vision bright, with colors true.
In failures past, we stitch and mend,
The broken parts, our hearts defend.

Each piece reflects a story's arc,
In darkened days, we find a spark.
Through unity, we shape a whole,
A tapestry that warms the soul.

And though the cracks may seem so vast,
In every flaw, the choice is cast.
To rise as one, to shine anew,
In recovery, our joys break through.

So gather 'round, this canvas wide,
Let's build a world where love abides.
For in the mess, we find our grace,
Recovering the piece we embrace.

## Whispers of Fractured Light

In twilight's embrace, shadows dance,
Fragments of dreams, a fleeting chance.
Stars flicker softly, secrets unfold,
Whispers of light in the night so cold.

Each gleam a story, intertwined fate,
Moments that linger, we hesitate.
Embers of hope in the heart's dim glow,
Guiding our paths where we dare not go.

Time gently ebbs, a river of sighs,
Crystals of laughter in tearful eyes.
Echoes of joy that fade into night,
Yet still we seek those whispers of light.

With every heartbeat, we mend the fray,
A tapestry woven through night and day.
Though shadows may linger, our spirits rise,
In whispers of fractured light, we find the skies.

## Shards of a Shattered Heart

Fractured pieces upon the floor,
Memories linger, they cut to the core.
Once whole and vibrant, now faded grey,
Love's gentle touch, lost along the way.

Each shard a whisper of what used to be,
Echoes of laughter, of you and me.
In the quiet moments, I hear the sound,
Of dreams now scattered, all around.

Reaching for solace, I gather the light,
Rebuilding the fragments, igniting the night.
In the depths of sorrow, I find my art,
Creating new beauty from this shattered heart.

Though wounds may ache and shadows may fight,
I cling to the hope hidden in the night.
With every heartbeat, I forge the start,
From the ashes, I rise with a brave heart.

## **Echoes of Resilience**

In the midst of chaos, strength takes flight,
Resilience blooms in the darkest night.
Through trials faced, the spirit grows,
Like wildflowers blooming where no one knows.

Echoes of courage resonate within,
Each challenge met, a battle to win.
With roots held firm in the fertile ground,
We rise unbroken, no longer bound.

In moments of doubt, we gather our flame,
Together we stand, forever the same.
Against the tide, we carry our dreams,
In unity's bond, nothing's as it seems.

So let the storms rage, let the tempest roar,
With hearts aligned, we shatter the door.
Through echoes of resilience, we shall soar,
Emerging anew, we are evermore.

## **Beneath the Cracks**

Where light seeps in through fractured seams,
Hope resides in the quiet beams.
Beneath the surface, stories unfold,
In hidden places, courage is bold.

Each crack a whisper of lessons learned,
Of bridges crossed and tides returned.
In the shadows cast by doubt's embrace,
Grows the strength that time cannot erase.

With every heartbeat, we mend the lines,
Planting the roots where the sun still shines.
For beneath the cracks lies fertile ground,
In the heart of the struggle, love can be found.

Together we venture, hand in hand tight,
Through the storms of sorrow, we find our light.
Beneath the cracks, hope's song softly calls,
In this fragile beauty, we rise through it all.

## **Shadows and Silhouettes**

In the dim light they dance,
Whispers of the past,
Figures glide like water,
Lost in shadows cast.

Lines entwine like fate,
A tapestry of night,
Silhouettes in silence,
Fading from our sight.

Fingers tracing memories,
On walls of ancient time,
Echoes fill the corners,
In a rhythmic chime.

Beneath the moon's soft gaze,
Stories intertwine,
Shadows hold their secrets,
In a world divine.

So let the darkness cradle,
What the light can't hold,
In shadows, find your courage,
In silhouettes, be bold.

## **Mosaic of Memories**

Fragments of our laughter,
Tiles of joy and pain,
Together they create,
A picture of our gain.

Each moment is a piece,
Colorful and bright,
Interwoven stories,
In the tapestry of light.

Time spills like a river,
Gathering the days,
Building up the layers,
In countless, winding ways.

Captured in the mosaic,
Every shard a spark,
Light reflects the past,
In shadows, there's a mark.

Now we stand together,
With memories in hand,
A beautiful mosaic,
A life that's truly planned.

**Embracing the Fallen**

Leaves drift down like whispers,
Carrying the chill,
Nature's gentle sighs,
Echo through the will.

Golden hues of autumn,
Cradled by the breeze,
Each fallen leaf a story,
Written with such ease.

Underneath the branches,
We gather all the dreams,
Embracing every moment,
In sunlight's golden beams.

As seasons turn and soften,
The world begins to fade,
Yet in the soft decay,
Life's beauty is displayed.

So let us hold the fallen,
Within our tender hands,
For in each quiet ending,
A new beginning stands.

## **The Resilient Bloom**

In cracks of stone it rises,
A stubborn, hopeful sprout,
Defying every winter,
With roots that twist about.

Petals brush the soft air,
Colors bold and bright,
A testament to spirit,
In the morning light.

Through storms and harshest weather,
It bends, but does not break,
A vision wrapped in courage,
With every chance it takes.

In gardens filled with shadows,
It stands, so proud and strong,
A miracle of nature,
In the world, we belong.

So let us learn from blooms,
That rise with grace and zest,
For in the heart of struggle,
Lies the spirit's quest.

## **Treasures in the Ruins**

Amidst the stones, a glimmer seen,
Whispers of tales in shades of green.
Lost hopes buried in the dust,
Golden dreams turned into rust.

Echoes of laughter in the air,
Shadows dance, a wondrous flair.
Through broken walls, we seek and find,
Remnants of a world intertwined.

Once vibrant gardens, now laid bare,
Petals scattered, memories rare.
In every crevice, stories sing,
Breath of life that past does bring.

Beneath the rubble, treasures gleam,
Fragments of a lost, sweet dream.
With open eyes, the heart perceives,
In ruins, the spirit believes.

Time's gentle hand can heal the scars,
From shattered earth, we reach for stars.
In the quiet, listen well,
For in the ruins, treasures dwell.

# Stitching the Heart

Threads of sorrow, woven tight,
Stitches made in silent night.
With each pull, a story grows,
A tapestry of joy and woes.

Needle dances, puncturing pain,
A quilt of hope, a doubling gain.
Heartbeats echo in the seam,
Together we mend, together we dream.

Frayed edges whisper tales of old,
Warming hands when life is cold.
In every knot, a lesson bound,
In fragile moments, strength is found.

Love's embrace, a gentle thread,
Wrapped around the words unsaid.
Stitch the heart with care and grace,
Creating beauty in the space.

As time unfolds, our stories blend,
Threads of life, we twist and bend.
In the stitching, find the art,
Of healing, growth, and a united heart.

## Cries of the Crumpled

Beneath the weight, a fragile sigh,
Whispers of dreams that fluttered by.
Crumpled papers tell their tale,
Silent battles that grew pale.

In quiet corners, shadows dwell,
Every wrinkle holds a spell.
Page by page, the truth unfolds,
In the crumpled, a heart of gold.

Muffled cries of hopes reborn,
In twisted forms, new paths are worn.
Every crease a story writes,
In the darkness, a spark ignites.

Lost in chaos, yet still alive,
Crumpled voices begin to strive.
Through the mess, a vision clear,
From tangled thoughts, we persevere.

In the fragile, beauty lies,
Lift the paper, watch it rise.
Crumpled hopes, we will not hide,
In every tear, our dreams abide.

## A Symphony of Cracks

Cracks across the canvas spread,
Letting light where dark once tread.
Drawn in silence, a melody,
Each fracture sings a mystery.

Notes of laughter, tears, and time,
Rust and gold in perfect rhyme.
In fragile moments, strength is found,
Resonating from the ground.

Every crevice, a chorus calls,
Echoes linger in ancient walls.
The symphony of life's embrace,
A harmony of love and grace.

Hear the whispers in the night,
Cracks of heart, a guiding light.
In shattered dreams, we find our song,
Together, we have always belonged.

From brokenness, the beauty swells,
In all the cracks, the spirit dwells.
Let the music fill the air,
In every crack, we lay our care.

## **Wings of the Crippled**

In shadows cast by silent grace,
A spirit soars, a fragile face.
Through broken dreams, it finds the light,
With tattered wings, it takes to flight.

Whispers of hope haunt the air,
A song of strength beyond despair.
Each flutter tells of battles won,
A journey bold, a heart unstrung.

Beneath the weight of heavy chains,
Resilience blooms through aches and pains.
A dance of courage, slow and strong,
The crippled wings still sing their song.

In the fractures, beauty grows,
A canvas made from life's throes.
With every scar, a tale to weave,
Of battles fought, of love believed.

And when the world feels cold and stark,
Remember well the ember's spark.
For wings may break, yet spirits rise,
In every tear, a hope replies.

## Paths Forged in Fracture

In the rubble, stories lie,
Paths that bend and twist up high.
Each crack a trail, each scar a guide,
Forging strength where fears abide.

Beneath the weight of heavy stones,
Resilience sings in whispered tones.
Through jagged edges, grace will bloom,
In broken places, life finds room.

Worn and weary, yet still we tread,
On paths where angels fear to tread.
With each new step, the heart ignites,
In fractured lands, our spirit fights.

The journey's hard, the shadows long,
But in the struggle, we grow strong.
With every fall, we learn to rise,
In fractured paths, we see the skies.

And so we walk, hand in hand,
Through every fracture, a promised land.
With courage fierce, we find our way,
Together strong, come what may.

## **Ink from the Wounds**

Ink spills forth from wounds unhealed,
Stories of battles, truth revealed.
Each drop a whisper from the past,
Ink from the wounds, shadows cast.

With trembling hands, we write the pain,
Transforming sorrow into gain.
Through verses flows a healing stream,
In every line, a distant dream.

The parchment holds our deepest fears,
Yet in the ink, we find our tears.
Each page a testament to fight,
Turning darkness into light.

The scars we bear, they weave our tale,
In every struggle, we will prevail.
With ink and heart, we paint our fate,
From wounds of love, we will create.

So let it flow, this ink of life,
Through joy and sorrow, peace and strife.
For in these wounds, our art takes flight,
Ink from the wounds, a guiding light.

## **Revelations in Ruin**

In ruins old, where secrets lie,
Revelations whisper to the sky.
Among the stones, the stories breathe,
In every crack, a truth we weave.

The remnants speak of love and loss,
In silent echoes, we bear the cross.
Through shattered dreams, the heart still seeks,
In whispered tales, the past still speaks.

Through crumbled walls, hope finds a way,
In every ruin, a brighter day.
Each broken piece, a lesson learned,
From ashes cold, a fire burned.

And so we walk on hallowed ground,
In every silence, wisdom found.
With open hearts, we dare to face,
The revelations time won't erase.

In the shadows of what once was grand,
We find the strength to take a stand.
For in the ruin, life anew,
Revelations shine, the dawn breaks through.

## Songs of the Shattered

In the echoes of the night,
Dreams once bright take flight.
Whispers of a broken heart,
Melodies that tear apart.

Fragments of a silent scream,
Crumbling beneath the gleam.
Every note, a mournful cry,
As the stars begin to die.

A melody of loss and grief,
Yearning for some kind of relief.
Chords that resonate with pain,
Finding solace in the rain.

Yet from the ashes, hope will rise,
In the shadows, light defies.
Songs of strength, we learn to sing,
Wounds that time will gently bring.

So let the shattered voices soar,
Healing through each opened door.
Together in this sacred space,
With love, we will embrace.

## **Resilience in the Abyss**

In the depths where shadows creep,
Silent vows and dreams we keep.
Each moment feels like endless night,
Yet deep within, we find the light.

Facing fears that pull us down,
Building strength without a crown.
Waves may crash, the storm may roar,
But through the tides, we learn to soar.

Hope ignites within the dark,
A flicker, then a vital spark.
And in this void, we feel alive,
With every breath, we start to thrive.

We rise again from broken dreams,
Life is more than what it seems.
Forged in trials, strong and bold,
With every story, we unfold.

Resilience blooms like a flower,
In haunting nights, we find our power.
Together, we fight, we stand tall,
In unity, we conquer all.

## Growth Amidst the Chaos

In swirling storms, we find our way,
Through tangled roots, we bend and sway.
Nature's grip may hold us tight,
Yet in the chaos, seeds take flight.

Each droplet falls, a lesson learned,
From flames of struggle, passion burned.
We rise anew, the soil rich,
Transforming wounds into our niche.

Chaos may shatter the silent ground,
But in the mess, our strength is found.
With every fall, we gather grace,
In life's wild dance, we find our place.

Roots entwined in troubled earth,
We nurture dreams of rebirth.
From cracks, we blossom, fierce and true,
Growth amidst the chaos we pursue.

In vibrant hues, the wildflowers bloom,
Shining brave against the gloom.
With every heartbeat, we declare,
In chaos, life is ours to share.

## Fragments of a Hidden Soul

In shadows cast by silent dreams,
Layers wrapped in secret schemes.
Whispers float on brittle air,
Truth concealed in tender care.

A puzzle formed of broken parts,
A tapestry of hidden hearts.
Each piece tells a story old,
In fragments, wisdom unfolds.

Beneath the surface, layers hide,
A world where secrets gently bide.
Echoes of laughter, tears of pain,
Every moment etched in grain.

Yet in the quiet, we reveal,
The beauty of what's truly real.
Through shattered glass, light will stream,
Unveiling fragments of our dream.

And as we mend our fractured whole,
We dance to songs of the soul.
Embracing all, both dark and bright,
In fragments, we find our light.

# Eclipsed Light

In shadows deep where silence sighs,
Hope flickers dim beneath dark skies.
Yet through the gloom a spark ignites,
Whispers of dawn, soft and bright.

Stars hidden by the moon's embrace,
Waiting to show their radiant face.
Each heartbeat echoes courage's call,
Eclipsed light will never fall.

With every dusk, a promise lies,
That darkness fades, the sun will rise.
Through trials faced, we learn to stand,
In unity, we lend a hand.

Embrace the night, with all its fears,
For in the dark, we sharpen years.
A tapestry of strength we weave,
In eclipsed light, we shall believe.

The universe holds secrets vast,
In shadows past, we find our cast.
Together we shall write our fate,
Transform the dark, and celebrate.

## **Tattered Pages of Existence**

Old books lie worn, their edges frayed,
Stories of life, both bright and shade.
Every page a chapter spun,
Tales of battles lost and won.

Ink stains the hearts of those who yearn,
Lessons learned, from each page turned.
The whispers of time echo soft,
In tattered pages, dreams lift off.

Memories linger, like a scent,
In faded lines, the heart is pent.
What was lost, now found in words,
Every silence, a song heard.

Dust settles on the fading lore,
Yet the spirit seeks to explore.
From broken lines, hope starts to rise,
In tattered pages, the soul flies.

Embrace the scars that shape our tale,
For in the cracks, love will prevail.
Through ink and time, we find our way,
In life's book, we choose to stay.

## **Threads of Resilience**

In the fabric of life, threads intertwine,
Colors blend, and destinies align.
Each moment a stitch, both strong and frail,
Weaving stories that will not pale.

Through trials faced, we find our thread,
With every tear, a patch is shed.
In the tapestry of love and strife,
Together, we thread the needles of life.

With hands outstretched, we mend the seams,
Transform our fears into radiant dreams.
Though frayed at times, our fabric holds,
In unity, our narrative unfolds.

Resilience blooms where chaos reigns,
From every loss, a lesson gains.
Through winding paths, we learn to grow,
In threads of resilience, the spirit glows.

So gather the strands, both bright and torn,
In the quilt of existence, we are reborn.
Embrace the strength, let laughter prevail,
In the weave of our hearts, we shall not fail.

## The Phoenix Within

From ashes grey, a flicker starts,
A tale of flame that stirs the hearts.
In darkest nights, it longs to soar,
The phoenix whispers, 'Rise once more.'

Through trials deep, and tempests wild,
The soul ignites, a fiery child.
Each struggle faced, a feather gained,
In the dance of fire, no fears remain.

Embrace the heat, let passion guide,
From every fall, the strength inside.
With wings of hope, and spirit free,
We rise anew, just wait and see.

In vibrant hues, we find our place,
A vivid tapestry of grace.
From pain transformed, we light the night,
In the heart of darkness, we'll find our light.

So hear the call, let courage flow,
For within each soul, the phoenix glows.
From embers cold, life takes its flight,
We are the fire, we are the light.

**Souls in Dissonance**

Whispers clash in silent night,
Dreams collide without a fight.
Strangers stand on fractured ground,
Harmony is seldom found.

Voices blend, a bitter song,
Loneliness where we belong.
Tales of love and pain entwined,
Echoes lost, we search for kind.

Fragile hearts seek meaning clear,
Yet the truth brings only fear.
Hope hangs on a fragile thread,
As the shadows swirl and spread.

Each emotion fights for space,
Yearning hearts begin to race.
Tangled paths we walk anew,
Searching for a love that's true.

In the silence, bonds are made,
Through the hurt, we are displayed.
Souls that yearn to break apart,
Finding solace in the dark.

## **Colors of the Unbroken**

Brush strokes dance on canvas bright,
Each hue speaks in pure delight.
Crimson red and azure blue,
Palette formed from every hue.

Golden rays that warm the soul,
Mixing shades to make us whole.
Emerald fields where whispers play,
Nature's art in grand display.

Tints of sorrow, shades of grace,
All reflected in this space.
Violet dreams and silvery light,
Crafting beauty, banishing night.

In the vibrant tapestry,
Life unfolds so endlessly.
Each moment a brush in hand,
Creating joy where we now stand.

Together we create the scene,
Painting life in colors keen.
Through the storms, we won't lose sight,
In our hearts, the colors bright.

## Echoes of the Past

Shadows linger where we tread,
Whispers of the words unsaid.
Faded echoes call our name,
Memory's fleeting, haunting flame.

Time stands still; we hear the sound,
Footsteps lost, yet still profound.
In each heartbeat lies the key,
Unlocking chains of history.

Photographs in sepia hues,
Reminding us of paths we choose.
Lost embraces, fleeting glance,
Time distorts a lover's dance.

Yet through the pain, a thread remains,
Binding joy and sorrow's strains.
Lessons learned in love and loss,
Forging strength through every cross.

So we walk the winding road,
Carrying the past's great load.
With each step, we forge ahead,
With echoes of the lives we've led.

## Maps of Scarred Paths

Worn and weathered, maps unfold,
Stories carved in lines of gold.
Each scar tells a tale so true,
Navigating paths we knew.

Markers guide us through the night,
Leading hearts toward the light.
Every bend a choice we make,
Lessons learned through love or ache.

In this journey, we find grace,
Revealing strengths that time can trace.
Wounds become a badge of pride,
As we navigate the tide.

Unraveled maps, yet still we seek,
Bravery in every peak.
Through the storms and darkest hours,
We rise anew, reclaiming powers.

So let us walk these paths once more,
Finding hope on every shore.
In the scars, a history vast,
We chart our futures from the past.

## Blossoms in the Ashes

In the shadows where embers lay,
Petals bloom, the night turns day.
Whispers of life in silent cries,
Hope emerges, the heart defies.

Amidst the grief, new colors rise,
Graceful arches paint the skies.
Strength in beauty, fierce and bold,
Fragrant stories waiting to be told.

From scorched earth, a tender seed,
Promises born from every need.
In fractured ground, the roots go deep,
Awakening dreams from endless sleep.

Gentle hands will tend the flame,
Each new blossom, a whispered name.
Love will linger, fierce and brave,
In the ashes, we learn to save.

Together we'll dance on fragile ground,
In the chaos, our souls unbound.
Blossoms thriving, hearts take flight,
In the ashes, we find our light.

## **Heartstrings Unraveled**

Tangled threads weave tales of old,
Songs of love and secrets told.
In the silence, echoes cling,
Melodies lost, yet slowly sing.

Whispers softly, the night's embrace,
Unraveling time, a slow-paced race.
Heartstrings tugged, a gentle pull,
Dreams entwined, both full and dull.

Through the cracks, light finds a way,
Guiding paths where shadows play.
Fragments scattered, yet we find,
Strength in love, forever blind.

Every note, a heartbeat's song,
In the rhythm, where we belong.
As the music weaves its art,
The unbroken binds the heart.

In the tapestry of joy and strife,
We mend the rifts, embrace our life.
Heartstrings linger, a sacred dance,
In the unraveling, we find our chance.

**Unveiling the Hidden Strength**


Beneath the surface, shadows wait,
Stories woven of fear and fate.
In the stillness, courage grows,
A force within that softly glows.

With each struggle, light breaks through,
Revealing paths, both bold and new.
Silent battles, fought each day,
Hidden strength will find a way.

Walls may crumble, hearts may shake,
From the ashes, we will wake.
In the silence, power calls,
Rising strong from shattered walls.

Embrace the scars that tell our tales,
In every storm, a spirit sails.
Unyielding hearts, we claim our right,
Boundless strength, the starry night.

So let us stand with heads held high,
Facing fears with every sigh.
Unveiling strength, fierce and grand,
In unity, we rise and stand.

## A Journey from Shatter to Shine

Fragmented dreams on the floor,
Each piece whispers, 'There's so much more.'
Through the broken, hope will gleam,
In the dark, we'll find our dream.

Steps may falter, paths may twist,
In the chaos, we still exist.
From the shatters, a light will grow,
Resilience born in the ebb and flow.

Every crack, a story shared,
Wounds that heal, and hearts prepared.
In the journey, strength defined,
From ashes left, bright futures find.

With every rise, a spark ignites,
Guiding us through anxious nights.
From shattered glass, a spirit soars,
In each fragment, open doors.

So take my hand, we'll walk this line,
Through every storm, our dreams align.
A journey forged from pain to grace,
In our hearts, we find our place.

## **Embracing the Imperfect**

In the cracks of our dreams, we find,
Beauty shaped by chaos, unconfined.
A canvas splashed with splinters of grace,
Tells tales of journeys we dare to embrace.

Flaws weave through our stories, so true,
Each scar a reminder of battles we knew.
In the quilt of existence, threads intertwine,
Creating a masterpiece, uniquely divine.

Beneath the weight of shame's heavy guard,
Lies the wisdom earned, though often hard.
With open hearts, we learn to perceive,
That perfect is merely a veil to believe.

So let us gather our pieces, unashamed,
Celebrate the paths that have shaped and claimed.
In the heart of the flawed, brilliance can shine,
Embracing the imperfect, our lives intertwine.

Together we dance, imperfectly bright,
In the embrace of our flaws, we ignite.
For in every misstep, a lesson we find,
In the tapestry woven, our spirits aligned.

## Dust to Dawn

Day meets night in a whispering breeze,
Carrying dreams from the deep, with ease.
Stars twinkle gently, a guiding array,
While shadows retreat as dusk turns to day.

The horizon blushes in colors so bold,
Promises of warmth in the sun's soft unfold.
Each moment a treasure, a second to reign,
Turning the dust of our fears into gain.

Whispers of dawn bring a fresh, sweet start,
Awakening hope in the deepest of hearts.
With every sunrise, we rise from the dark,
Embracing the light, igniting the spark.

Through trials that weigh like an old, heavy cloak,
We shed the past with each word that we spoke.
In the dance of the light, we shed every frown,
Transforming our spirits from dust to dawn.

So let the day break with promise anew,
As we stand together, refreshed and renewed.
With hope in our hands and dreams on the rise,
We embrace the bright future that greets us with skies.

## The Light Beneath the Scars

Beneath the layers of hurt, we find,
A glimmer of hope that softly entwined.
Each scar a story, a tale to be told,
Of battles surrendered and moments bold.

Like fireflies glowing in shadows of night,
The beauty within gives the heart its might.
In valleys of sorrow, where darkness may lie,
A flicker of light whispers, 'Here, you can fly.'

The past holds its lessons, both bitter and sweet,
With every scar earned, we rise to our feet.
Embracing our flaws, we learn to forgive,
For through our own wounds, the light begins to live.

So let every tear be a path to the stars,
Leading us closer, despite all the bars.
In the quilt of our being, stitched with love's thread,
Beneath every scar, brighter dreams can be spread.

We gather the fragments, a mosaic of grace,
Finding strength in the shadows, a luminous place.
With light shining through, our spirits can soar,
The light beneath scars reveals so much more.

# **Iridescent Fragments**

Scattered like jewels in the depths of the soul,
Iridescent fragments that make us feel whole.
Each piece reflects a life lived anew,
Shimmering colors of red, green, and blue.

From the ashes of heartache, we rise and we shine,
Woven together, our paths intertwine.
A tapestry woven with the threads of our fate,
Beauty in chaos, we learn to create.

Memories dance in the light of the day,
The shards of our stories, a vibrant array.
In the silence we find the songs yet unsung,
The whispers of hope on our hearts are still young.

We gather our fragments; we share our own light,
Illuminating each other through dark and through bright.
In loving connection, we find our true worth,
The iridescence of life, a celebration of birth.

So hold out your hands, let the colors collide,
Embrace every fragment, let love be our guide.
For in every reflection, we discover the core,
Iridescent fragments, forever we soar.

## **Blossoming Through the Cracks**

In stone and steel, life dares to bloom,
A tiny bud breaks through the gloom.
With tender touch, it claims the light,
A rebel heart in silent fight.

Roots weave through shadows, seeking grace,
Nature's will in a harsh place.
Petals unfurl with vibrant hue,
Defying odds, forever true.

Each crack a canvas, each fracture art,
Resilience painted upon the heart.
Through concrete jungles, flowers dare,
To rise up strong, to breathe the air.

Hope finds footing in the least,
In every struggle, life's released.
Amidst the chaos, joy can thrive,
A testament that we survive.

So when you stumble, don't despair,
Look for the blooms that linger there.
A thousand stories held in place,
Whispering strength, a warm embrace.

## **Unearthed Beauty**

Beneath the surface, treasures wait,
In quiet depths, life finds its fate.
With gentle hands, we brush away,
The layers thick, to find the play.

Roots intertwined with time and stone,
Where seeds of wisdom once were sown.
In hidden nooks, the flowers grow,
Revealing stories, soft and slow.

Each crack a portal to the past,
Unearthed beauty meant to last.
Glimmers of light in earthy tones,
Nature's canvas, dreams and bones.

With every shovel, we discover,
Life's sweet songs, like no other.
From soil and silence, we behold,
The vibrant past in colors bold.

Embrace the journey, take your time,
In every echo, hear the chime.
Unearthed beauty, forever free,
A precious gift for you and me.

## The Language of Fractures

In shattered lines and broken dreams,
Lies a language that softly screams.
Each crack a story, whispered loud,
In quiet corners, life is proud.

The heart of stone, a voice so clear,
In fractured spaces, we draw near.
From chaos born, a melody,
The sound of hope, a symphony.

Listen close, to tales they weave,
In every crease, a chance to grieve.
But through the pain, we find our way,
In fractured light, we choose to stay.

Sharp edges speak with gentle force,
Steering souls upon their course.
Through shattered moments, truths arise,
Reflecting strength in cloudy skies.

So when you find the world so cracked,
Remember, beauty's been unpacked.
With every fracture's tender trace,
Lives a story wrapped in grace.

## Wholeness from Whispers

In whispered notes on evening's breeze,
The world finds peace, as heart's at ease.
Each gentle sigh, a dance of air,
A quiet promise, life laid bare.

From fragments soft, we build anew,
In whispered dreams, our spirits grew.
With every breath, we weave the night,
A tapestry of dark and light.

Listen closely to the nightingale,
Her songs of hope will never fail.
In every hush, in each refrain,
A truth that whispers, love remains.

Wholeness found in shadows cast,
In every moment, hold it fast.
With every whisper, heart to heart,
Together rise, though worlds may part.

So sing the song of what could be,
In whispers woven, you and me.
From silence grows the loudest call,
In unity, we rise, not fall.

## Shapes of Silence

In shadowed corners, whispers rest,
Echoes of thoughts left unexpressed.
Shapes of silence, softly drawn,
Hiding truths till the break of dawn.

A stillness speaks where voices cease,
Finding solace in quiet peace.
Frames of moments, lost in time,
Crafting tales in subtle rhyme.

The air is thick with unformed dreams,
Stitched together with silent seams.
Where eyes converse and hearts ignite,
A tapestry woven from endless night.

Shapes of silence, profound and wide,
Holding secrets we cannot hide.
In every pause, a world unfolds,
A magic place where silence holds.

And in this realm, we come alive,
In quiet spaces, our thoughts survive.
Embracing shadows, we dare to tread,
In shapes of silence, we find our thread.

## Luminescence of Loss

In the twilight where shadows grow,
Flickers of memory softly glow.
A luminescence that haunts the night,
Illuminating what once was bright.

Each tear a spark, each sigh a flame,
Rekindling love that still feels the same.
Echoes whisper through dim-lit halls,
Of laughter shared and distant calls.

In the quiet, a soft embrace,
Grief and beauty share their space.
Time stretches out, yet flies away,
In luminescence, we learn to stay.

The heart glows warm with hidden scars,
Each wound a light beneath the stars.
Through the pain, we begin to see,
The luminescence of what used to be.

Though loss may strike with heavy hand,
A fragile hope helps us to stand.
In the shadows, the light will cross,
We find our way through the luminescence of loss.

## Bridges from Brokenness

Across the chasms of heart's despair,
We fashion bridges with utmost care.
From shards of sorrow, strong and true,
We build our way with a hopeful view.

Each crack a story, every tear a sign,
A path emerges where we entwine.
In brokenness, we find our grace,
With every step, we write our place.

The rubble serves as stepping stones,
Leading us through the pain we've known.
Hand in hand, we walk the line,
Building bridges, your heart and mine.

Through stormy skies and rivers wide,
Together we'll journey, side by side.
From brokenness, we rise and soar,
Crafting bridges to forevermore.

In every fissure, a chance to grow,
Through the darkness, a gentle glow.
Bridges from brokenness lead to light,
Transforming shadows into flight.

## Silent Roars of the Heart

Within the chambers, silence cries,
A roar that echoes, deep and wise.
In shadows thick, where feelings dwell,
The heart sends messages we can't tell.

Beneath the surface, turmoil brews,
A symphony of unspoken hues.
Each heartbeat drums a tale of strife,
Silent roars shape the pulse of life.

An unseen tempest stirs the soul,
Waves of emotion, vast and whole.
In silence, we learn to rise and fall,
Roaring inside, we stand tall.

The whispers of hope amidst the pain,
In every silence, we find the gain.
The language of hearts, raw and real,
Silent roars reveal what we feel.

Through the quiet, we gather our strength,
A fierce resilience, boundless in length.
In silent roars of the heart, we find,
A voice that echoes through space and time.

**Beyond the Wounds**

In the silence where pain breathes,
Whispers of courage find the light.
Scars fade but stories linger,
Hope blooms in the softest night.

Each tear a river, flowing free,
Carving paths where dreams might tread.
With every step, the heart finds peace,
Beyond the wounds, love is spread.

Step by step through haunted halls,
Memories dance like shadows long.
In the cracks, new flowers rise,
Their fragrance sings a healing song.

The journey bends but does not break,
Resilience roots in steadfast ground.
Through stormy skies, and quiet tears,
The strength of spirit knows no bounds.

So here we stand, with open hands,
Embracing what the past can teach.
For in the depths of every fall,
Are wings of hope that rise and reach.

## **Love in the Chasms**

In the chasms of the heart,
A flicker ignites the dark.
Love whispers soft, a gentle art,
Healing wounds like a tender spark.

Between the echoes and the cries,
Silent promises begin to weave.
Each thread a bond that never dies,
In the quiet, we learn to believe.

Through shadows deep and caverns wide,
We traverse with hands entwined tight.
In every doubt, love is our guide,
Illuminating the ghosts of night.

When doubt looms like a heavy cloud,
Love's warmth can break the chill.
In shared laughter or a sigh aloud,
We find strength in the stillness, still.

So let us wander, hand in hand,
Through chasms where our spirits soar.
In love's embrace, we understand,
Together, we are forevermore.

## A Journey Among the Splinters

Among the splinters, we walk slow,
Every stumble, a lesson learned.
In jagged paths, our shadows grow,
Yet in the light, our hearts have burned.

With every step, the echoes call,
Reminders of the roads we've crossed.
Resilience blooms where we might fall,
Hope glimmers bright, never lost.

The world is wild, a precious maze,
We navigate, unsure but bold.
In tangled roots, we find our gaze,
With every story, we unfold.

Through bruises and triumphs, we will thrive,
In the dance of pain and grace.
Each splinter whispers, we're alive,
In this journey, we find our place.

So let us cherish every scar,
A testament to battles won.
Among the splinters, there you are,
Together, merging into one.

## **Patterns of Resilience**

In the fabric of our days,
Threads of strength intertwine.
With each challenge, life conveys,
Resilience dances, bold and fine.

Patterns crafted through the years,
Woven by hands both frail and strong.
In every smile, and through the tears,
We learn the words to our own song.

The storms may roar, the winds may howl,
Yet beneath the chaos, hope stands tall.
In the quiet, we lift our vow,
Together, we can face it all.

Through broken paths and haunted roads,
We gather pieces, stitch by stitch.
In each story, a treasure grows,
Resilience teaches us to switch.

So here's to those who fight and stand,
Lessons learned, with courage bound.
In patterns rich, our lives expand,
In resilience, true love is found.

## Lights in the Abyss

In the depths where shadows weave,
Flickers dance, hope to relieve.
Stars above in silent cheer,
Guiding souls who wander near.

Whispers echo through the night,
Promises of dawning light.
Clarity in chaos found,
As dreams rise from hollow ground.

Courage blooms in darkest times,
While the heart begins to climb.
Each glimmer feeds the soul's fire,
Reaching high, we'll never tire.

Through the void, we find our way,
Chasing shadows, come what may.
In the silence, voices plead,
For the light, our hearts will heed.

So we rise and break the chains,
From the depths where sorrow reigns.
Together, we will face the strife,
Finding strength in every life.

## Harmony from Havoc

In the midst of storms that rage,
We find peace, unlock the cage.
Melodies in chaos blend,
Turning darkness to a friend.

With each clash, a rhythm starts,
Dancing echoes of our hearts.
Bridges formed from shattered dreams,
Building hope from broken seams.

Let the dissonance resound,
In its depths, true strength is found.
Life's a song with bitter notes,
Yet, through struggle, spirit floats.

Weaving joy in threads of pain,
Through the drought, the thirst for rain.
From the ashes, colors rise,
Painting truths beneath the skies.

In the whispers, listen close,
Softly speaking what we chose.
Moments fleeting, we embrace,
Creating harmony in space.

## The Art of Disarray

Scattered pieces on the floor,
Tell a tale, then open doors.
Chaos swirls, a vibrant scene,
In the mess, a life unseen.

Fractured thoughts like shattered glass,
Reflect the light as moments pass.
Each misstep, a wild brush,
Crafting art in every rush.

Colors clash and patterns fight,
Yet they weave a cloth of light.
In the clutter, beauty grows,
Life's a canvas, truth bestows.

With the blurs, our stories speak,
In the midst of strong and weak.
Finding grace in what we lack,
Painting paths we can't turn back.

Embrace the chaos, let it be,
In disarray, we start to see.
Life's true art—a messy guise,
Emerging from the tangled ties.

## Navigating the Maze

Life's a labyrinth, twists and turns,
In its heart, the spirit yearns.
Every corner, secrets hide,
Paths of fate we must abide.

With the map drawn on the soul,
We traverse, seeking the whole.
Guided by the inner light,
Shadows flicker, hint of night.

Through the walls, on whispers glide,
Finding strength we hold inside.
Every obstacle, a test,
Breaking through, we seek the rest.

In the silence, answers bloom,
Turning fear to sweet perfume.
Through the trials, wisdom grows,
Teaching us what life bestows.

As we wander, hearts awake,
Every step to learn, not fake.
Navigating, bold and brave,
We will find what hearts can save.

## The Heart's Resilience

In shadows deep, hearts learn to mend,
A whispered hope, a trusted friend.
Through storms that rage and winds that wail,
The spirit stands, refused to pale.

With every tear, a lesson flows,
From pain that cuts, true strength grows.
In silence, strength finds its way,
To greet the dawn of a brighter day.

Each scar a tale, a courage shared,
A mark of love, of how we cared.
As roots hold firm against the strife,
Resilience blooms, the gift of life.

In courage's grip, we rise anew,
With open hearts, we journey through.
The heart endures, it builds, it grows,
In every trial, true strength shows.

So let the winds of change now blow,
For in the storm, our spirit glows.
For every challenge, grace will find,
The heart's resilience, forever blind.

## Light in the Twilight

As day gives way to evening's grace,
A soft embrace, a warm embrace.
The twilight glows, the stars ignite,
In gentle whispers, the world feels right.

The colors blend in soft delight,
As shadows dance and fade from sight.
A moment's peace, a fleeting glance,
The heart takes wing in twilight's dance.

With every breath, a magic born,
In twilight's glow, a new dawn sworn.
The world transforms in golden hue,
Each step a chance, a dream come true.

In the quiet, our hopes reside,
The magic found when dreams collide.
Through ebbing light, our spirits soar,
In twilight's arms, we wish for more.

So hold the light, let moments last,
For every twilight is a glimpse of vast.
In every heart, a flame can spark,
To guide through night, illuminate the dark.

## **Vessels of Change**

In every heart, a vessel waits,
To carry dreams, to shift the fates.
With opened sails, we brave the seas,
Embracing winds, feeling the breeze.

No course too tough, no wave too high,
With courage strong, we glide and fly.
Through shifting tides, we find our way,
Each challenge faced, a brand new day.

With strength in numbers, hand in hand,
We navigate, we take a stand.
For every journey shapes our soul,
As vessels find their destined goal.

Through storms we rise, through calm we grow,
Each twist and turn, a chance to flow.
The compass guides, the stars align,
In every heart, potential shines.

So trust the journey, cherish the change,
For life's a dance, both wild and strange.
As vessels flow, our stories blend,
Together we craft the journey's end.

## Touching the Twisted Threads

In woven lives where tales entwine,
We touch the threads, a sacred sign.
With every knot, a bond we share,
In tangled paths, we find our care.

Each color speaks in shades of truth,
Of time and love, of pain and youth.
With open hands, we weave our fate,
In every twist, new paths await.

The fabric rich with dreams untold,
In every stitch, the heart feels bold.
Through storms we craft, through light we play,
In every fiber, hope will stay.

So hug the frays and mend the weak,
For in these threads, our voices seek.
To touch the hearts of those we know,
And weave a life where kindness grows.

Through tangled dreams, we find our way,
In every thread, a chance to sway.
Together we stand, a tapestry bright,
Touching the threads, we find our light.

## Mending the Fragments

Shattered dreams lie in a heap,
Hope's remnants buried, far too deep.
With tender hands, I start to mold,
Piecing stories, brave and bold.

Time's gentle threads weave through the night,
Stitching shadows, sparking light.
Each fragment holds a tale untold,
In brokenness, I find my gold.

Healing whispers kiss the scars,
Transforming wounds, like distant stars.
The heart learns to dance once more,
In every crack, love starts to soar.

Embrace the beauty, let it sing,
From shattered past, a new dawn springs.
Together, fragments will entwine,
In the light, they brightly shine.

Mending these pieces, I become whole,
In every crack resides a soul.
With every stitch, a promise made,
In love's soft hands, no dreams will fade.

## A Heart Deconstructed

In pieces lay my tender heart,
Each fragment sings its own sweet part.
A melody of joy and pain,
In chaos formed, I learn to gain.

What once was whole is now a song,
A structure built, yet not for long.
With every beat, reflection grows,
In shattered glass, the true heart glows.

Rebuilding walls with threads of grace,
I find my strength in this new space.
The cracks designed by hands of fate,
In vulnerability, I create.

Old layers shed, revealing light,
In every shadow, dreams ignite.
A heart deconstructed, whole again,
Reclaimed in love, I shall remain.

In echoes past, I find my way,
A tapestry of night and day.
Through whispered fears, resilient art,
I rise anew, a brave new start.

## Tattered Wings

Tattered wings, once bold in flight,
Now grounded low, seeking the night.
Yet in the stillness, courage grows,
From frayed edges, beauty flows.

Battered dreams hang on the line,
Hope's soft whisper, a gentle sign.
Embrace the lessons in the fall,
For flight begins when we hear the call.

With every tear, a story spun,
In quiet moments, we become one.
Wings may falter, spirits soar,
Through brokenness, we learn to roar.

Fragile hearts, we mend with care,
In every scar, a badge we wear.
Tattered wings, they dance and sway,
Finding strength in every fray.

In the ruins, we weave our dreams,
A tapestry stitched at the seams.
From the depths, we rise unchained,
With tattered wings, our souls reclaimed.

## **Whispers Among the Ruins**

Among the ruins, silence speaks,
A thousand stories, lost in streaks.
Echoes linger, soft and bright,
Whispers dance in the faded light.

Forgotten places, hearts connect,
In every shadow, we reflect.
Amidst the crumbling, hope remains,
In every crack, love's joy sustains.

Nature's breath caresses stone,
Life persists in the overthrown.
Hidden beauty blooms in decay,
A reminder that love finds a way.

Here in the ruins, we find our truth,
In every whisper, the voice of youth.
Healing happens in silence shared,
Connecting souls who once despaired.

These ancient walls, they hold our dreams,
In faded colors, life redeems.
Let whispers linger, gently guide,
Among the ruins, love will bide.

## The Beauty of What's Lost

In twilight's glow, shadows weave,
Memories dance, but we grieve.
Moments like petals blown away,
Fragile whispers of yesterday.

The heart retains what eyes can't see,
Silent echoes of what used to be.
A treasure trove of faded dreams,
Carried softly on moonlit streams.

Time's gentle hand will caress the past,
Love's essence captured, forever to last.
In sorrow's depth, a beauty lies,
In every goodbye, the soul will rise.

Through autumn leaves, we learn to find,
The beauty born of the intertwined.
In loss, we find a deeper grace,
A tender smile in a familiar face.

So hold the fragments, don't let them fade,
In the heart's garden, memories stayed.
For what is lost is never gone,
In love's embrace, we carry on.

## An Odyssey Among the Shards

Through broken glass and scattered light,
We journey forth into the night.
Each shard a tale, each cut a song,
A traveler's path where we belong.

With every step, the silence grows,
As whispers of the past compose.
Fragments shimmering under the stars,
Mapping journeys among the scars.

The heart of dreams, once whole and bright,
Now veiled in shadows, finding light.
Yet in the chaos, a beauty lies,
In shattered pieces, the spirit flies.

We gather strength from words unspoken,
In every break, a promise broken.
For every loss, a stepping stone,
An odyssey, we walk alone.

As dawn approaches, darkness sleeps,
Among the shards, a wisdom keeps.
Each piece a part of who we've been,
In brokenness, the hope will gleam.

## Healing the Treasures

In the quiet hours, a soft refrain,
Tender moments heal the pain.
Beneath the scars, the heart can grow,
Seeds of hope in gentle glow.

Time, the healer of all wounds,
Sings softly of its timeless tunes.
With every tear, the soul will mend,
In brokenness, new paths ascend.

Forgiveness weaves its golden thread,
Linking all the words unsaid.
In the light of dawn, we find our way,
Healing treasures in the fray.

The tapestry of life unfolds,
In every heart, a story holds.
Through shadows cast and doubts that place,
We rise anew with tender grace.

So cherish each moment, let them flow,
For healing treasures will surely grow.
In every scar, a tale so bright,
Reminders of love's enduring light.

## Unseen Pathways of Light

In the fog where whispers cling,
Unseen pathways begin to sing.
Through winding roads of doubt and fear,
Discern the truth when hearts are clear.

Each step reveals a silent grace,
Guiding souls to a cherished place.
In shadows deep, a spark ignites,
Unseen pathways of hidden lights.

The journey winds through starry skies,
Where hope is born and courage lies.
With every heartbeat, we draw near,
To unseen truths, both bold and sheer.

In the darkness, find the spark,
Embrace the journey, venture to embark.
For life unfolds in wondrous ways,
As unseen pathways light our days.

So take the first step, let go of fright,
Trust in the flow, into the light.
For every journey begins anew,
In unseen pathways, we will break through.

## **Harmony Within Discord**

In shadows deep where whispers play,
The clash of thoughts in disarray.
Yet from this chaos, beauty shines,
A symphony of tangled lines.

Fragmented voices, loud and clear,
Echoes dance, drawing us near.
In discord's heart, a spark ignites,
Uniting souls in starry nights.

The storm may rage, the winds may howl,
Yet within it, we find a prowl.
For in each clash, a truth unfurls,
In chaos, art, in peace, our worlds.

With hands entwined, we face the fight,
Embracing dark to seek the light.
In every struggle, love can grow,
Through harmony, the soul will glow.

Together we stand, through thick and thin,
In dissonance, we learn to spin.
From broken notes, a tune we craft,
In unity, our hearts are draft.

## The Elegance of Imperfection

A crooked line, a gentle curve,
In flaws, we find the heart's true verve.
Each scar tells stories, raw and real,
In shattered grace, we learn to heal.

The vase with cracks still holds the bloom,
Beauty emerges from the gloom.
In asymmetry, there's a dance,
A chance to find in loss, romance.

The art of life, a painted mess,
Each blemish whispers, 'You are blessed.'
With imperfections, we stand alone,
Yet find in them our perfect throne.

A patchwork heart, stitched with intent,
In every flaw, a smile is lent.
Together woven, a tale unfolds,
In our rough edges, love beholds.

So here we stand, in all our grace,
Uneven steps, a warm embrace.
In every crease, a lesson learned,
In elegance, our hearts are turned.

## **Finding Serenity in Shards**

Among the shards of what once was,
Lies stillness found in silent pause.
Each piece reflects a distant glow,
In brokenness, new pathways flow.

Shattered dreams can craft a view,
A mosaic bright, in colors true.
Every fragment tells a tale,
Of struggle, strength, and paths we hail.

In chaos dwells a quiet peace,
Where jagged edges slowly cease.
Embracing all that's left behind,
To seek the solace that we find.

Nature's grace in cracks appears,
Each void an echo of our fears.
Yet through the gaps, the light will beam,
In every shard, a hopeful dream.

Together we weave a healing thread,
In scattered pieces, no heart is dread.
Finding beauty in our scars,
In every brokenness, new stars.

## **Benedictions in the Broken**

In fractured spaces, blessings rise,
Where sorrow dwells, new hope defies.
With every bend and twisted fate,
A chance to love, a path to create.

Raindrops dance on cracked cement,
Each puddle holds a dream well-spent.
In brokenness, we grant reprieve,
From lesser chains, we learn to believe.

With open hearts, embracing pain,
In every storm, love's sweet refrain.
Through loss we find a light so bright,
In shadows cast, we seek the light.

Among the wreckage, kindness blooms,
In tender hearts, a cure for glooms.
In broken melodies, songs arise,
A choir of souls beneath the skies.

So let us gather every piece,
In shattered dreams, our love's increase.
Benedictions in the hollow,
For through the cracks, we learn to follow.

## **An Invitation to Heal**

In the quiet whispers of the night,
A gentle breeze brings hope's soft light.
Take a step, release the pain,
Find the peace that still remains.

Let the heartache fade away,
Embrace the dawn of a new day.
Each scar tells a story dear,
Invite the love, invite the cheer.

Together we will mend the seams,
Finding strength in shared dreams.
Hold my hand, don't look back,
We're on a bright, healing track.

Let the rivers of sorrow flow,
Cleanse the soul, let healing grow.
In the stillness, hear the call,
You're not alone, we rise, we fall.

With each breath, the past does wane,
In the light, we break the chain.
Join the dance of whispered grace,
In unity, we find our place.

## Shattered Reflections

Mirror fragments on the floor,
Each piece holds tales of yore.
Faces lost in time's embrace,
Searching for a familiar place.

When shadows deepen, truths collide,
Hidden fears we cannot hide.
In the shards, a glimpse of light,
Fading echoes of our fight.

What was whole is now a maze,
Wandering through a smoky haze.
In the darkness, find your glow,
In shattered parts, new paths will show.

Collect the pieces, one by one,
Embrace the self, let healing run.
Each scar a lesson, each crack a sign,
In the brokenness, we redefine.

Through the chaos, learn to see,
Beauty born from memory.
In reflections scattered, we shall find,
A tapestry of heart and mind.

## Fractured Light

Through the prism, colors burst,
In the shadows, a subtle thirst.
Chasing rays that dance and play,
In fractured light, we'll find our way.

Splintered beams that twist and turn,
In their glow, the soul will yearn.
Every hue, a tale re-spun,
From the darkness, we emerge as one.

In the colors, find your peace,
Let the chaos find its cease.
Through the cracks, the warmth will seep,
Guiding hearts toward the deep.

Songs of light in broken frame,
Echo in hearts, kindling flame.
From the shards, transformation grows,
In fractured light, a garden sows.

Let the spectrum heal your sight,
In the fractured, find the bright.
Hold the light, let shadows fade,
In this journey, love won't trade.

## Echoes of Dismay

In the stillness, whispers sigh,
Dismay dances, shadows lie.
Yet in sorrow, resilience blooms,
Amidst the fading, life resumes.

Hear the echoes, feel the weight,
In the silence, forge your fate.
From the ashes, rise anew,
Find the strength to see it through.

Moments linger, heavy and long,
Yet deep within, there brews a song.
Echoes fade, but not the pain,
Through the storm, we find our gain.

Take a breath, release the cry,
Search the horizon, paint the sky.
In the dismay, find the grace,
With every stumble, we embrace.

In the echoes, learn to stand,
In the dismay, reach for the hand.
Together we shall break the chains,
From the shadows, love remains.

## **Portraits of the Battered**

Shadows linger on weary skin,
Whispers of battles deep within.
Eyes that tell of storms they've braved,
Hearts once warm, now feeling enslaved.

Each scar a story, pain engraved,
In the silence, strength is saved.
They walk a path of broken light,
Carrying dreams through the night.

Hope flickers in a fading dusk,
Resilience rising from the husk.
In the cracks, beauty finds a way,
To shine through darkness, bright as day.

Memories haunt but do not define,
Every tear a fragile line.
On these canvases worn but true,
Stories of courage come into view.

Together they stand, hands held tight,
In the aftermath, they'll ignite.
From battered hearts a new beat plays,
Portraits alive in a dance of grace.

## **Vows to the Fractured**

Promises spoken in whispered breath,
Binding the lost in the face of death.
Against the odds, they take their stand,
With trembling hearts, they join their hands.

In the dark, they carve their reign,
Declaring love will not be in vain.
Fingers entwined, they face the fight,
Vows echo softly in the night.

Through fractured dreams and broken paths,
They navigate both joy and wrath.
For every scar, a story shared,
In the shadows, love declared.

With every heartbeat, deeper ties,
Trust emerges as hope defies.
In pieces, they'll find new strengths,
Together they'll measure life's lengths.

For vows are not mere words exchanged,
But lifelines drawn when hope is strained.
In unity, they rise anew,
Fractured yet whole, vibrant and true.

## Roots in the Ruins

In the rubble where silence reigns,
Life emerges from the strains.
Roots dig deep in shattered ground,
From desolation, hope is found.

Through the cracks, green tendrils creep,
Whispers of life in shadows steep.
They reach for light, defy the gloom,
Blooming brightly from the tomb.

Each petal holds a legacy,
Of resilience in a symphony.
Nature's will cannot be quelled,
In every heart, the seed is held.

Amidst the ruins, stories thrive,
Proof that beauty stays alive.
With every storm, tenacity grows,
Fractured earth, yet life bestows.

From ashes, they build and grow anew,
Roots intertwining, fierce and true.
In the bittersweet, they find their way,
In the ruins, a brighter day.

## Navigating Splintered Dreams

In the chaos of the night,
Dreams wander, seeking light.
Shattered visions scatter wide,
Yet deep within, hopes confide.

Through twisted paths, they find their course,
Fuelled by an inner force.
Each fragment tells a tale untold,
Of brave hearts and spirits bold.

Navigating through the dreamless void,
The lost and weary, hope employed.
With every step, they stitch and mend,
The shattered truth that they defend.

In the splinters, beauty thrives,
Echoes of life, where courage drives.
For every fracture, a light prevails,
In navigating through the trails.

Together they dance on shards of glass,
Learning to let each moment pass.
With hearts aligned, they'll weave a stream,
Navigating towards a shared dream.

## Embracing the Splinters

In shadows cast by fading light,
We learn to dance with unseen fright.
Each splinter tells a tale of grace,
A scarred heart finds its rightful place.

With trembling hands, we touch the pain,
In brokenness, we find the gain.
Through every crack, the light shines through,
Embracing all that makes us true.

A mosaic of our dreams at play,
In fragments, we find our own way.
Together, we stitch the past anew,
With colors vibrant, bold, and true.

Though at times the road feels steep,
In the silence, secrets sleep.
We gather strength from every fall,
In splinters, we discover all.

So let us weave, with hands so fine,
A tapestry of yours and mine.
For in the cracks, love's light can gleam,
In splinters, we find hope's sweet dream.

## **From Ruins Rise**

In echoes of what once stood tall,
We hear the whispers of the fall.
Yet in the dust, new dreams ignite,
From ashes, we reclaim our flight.

Each brick a story, each stone a seed,
From shattered past, we gently heed.
With hope as fire and love as light,
We carve our path into the night.

From ruins scattered, life will bloom,
In darkness strong, we find our room.
With every heartbeat, we rebuild,
From broken chains, our spirits thrilled.

The past may linger, shadows cast,
Yet we will not be shaped by glass.
With hands entwined, we rise above,
In unity, we find our love.

So let the world see what we can do,
Transforming loss, creating anew.
Among the rubble, flowers thrive,
From ruins deep, we rise alive.

# Tides of Transformation

The ocean breathes in rhythmic waves,
Each swell a story, each tide it saves.
From tranquil shores to tempest's roar,
We ride the currents, seek the shore.

In whispers soft, the waters say,
Change is the dance of night and day.
What once was lost will find its way,
A journey anew, come what may.

With every twist, the sea unfolds,
In depths unknown, new worlds behold.
We shed the past like shells so light,
Embracing waves, welcoming night.

The tides will rise, and tides will fall,
Yet through it all, we stand so tall.
For storms may come, but hope remains,
In transformation, love sustains.

So let us flow, like rivers blend,
Into the vastness, we ascend.
Through tides that churn and storms that call,
In transformation, we rise from all.

## The Art of Mending

In gentle hands, we start to weave,
A fabric where the heart believes.
With every stitch, a promise made,
In mending wounds, our fears will fade.

The threads of hope, like silken light,
Entwine our sorrows, banish night.
In tender care, we find the way,
Through the art of mending, come what may.

With needle poised, we draw the line,
Across the rips, our spirits shine.
For every tear is but a chance,
To dance again, to love, to prance.

Though scars may linger, stories told,
They weave a tapestry of bold.
In every patch, our truths unfold,
The art of mending, worth more than gold.

So let us cherish what we repair,
In love and light, we breathe the air.
For in the stitches, the soul shall find,
The art of mending, beautifully intertwined.

## Reverberations of the Heart

In the stillness of the night,
Whispers echo soft and bright.
Promises made under the stars,
Carried forth on gentle bars.

Feel the pulse, the warmth, the glow,
Time weaves tales of joy and woe.
Each heartbeat sings a song of old,
Cradled dreams in hands of gold.

Moments dance like shadows cast,
Fleeting whispers of the past.
Love's vibration, a sweet refrain,
In its echo, we find pain.

Through the valleys, highs, and lows,
Resilience in the heart that knows.
As the night gives way to dawn,
Hope's reverberations carry on.

Every beat, a step we take,
Together, hearts begin to wake.
In their rhythm, we are one,
Unraveling 'til the song is done.

## Silence of the Splintered Soul

In the shadows where echoes dwell,
A broken heart, a silent well.
Fragments whisper in the gloom,
Yearning stillness, heavy room.

Each shard reflects a part once whole,
A flickering flame within the soul.
Lost in thought, beneath the stars,
We trace our lives and bear the scars.

The silence speaks, a language raw,
In cracks and fissures, we withdraw.
Echoes linger, unraveling time,
A fragile heart, a muted rhyme.

Yet in the depths, a soft refrain,
Hope unfurls, like blooms after rain.
Through the cracks, a light appears,
Guiding us beyond our fears.

With each breath, we begin to mend,
Reclaiming voices, hearts ascend.
From silence born, we find our say,
Healing souls that gently sway.

## The Grace of Healing Hands

In tender touch, the world can change,
A gentle strength, both soft and strange.
Fingers weave through pain and strife,
Bringing warmth back to our life.

With every gesture, hope ignites,
A dance of shadows, soothing lights.
Hands that hold, both firm and free,
Crafting pathways to what can be.

Through the turmoil of despair,
Lies the promise of repair.
Embracing wounds with loving care,
Healing whispers fill the air.

Wherever broken spirits lie,
Hands extend to mend and tie.
In their grace, we find our way,
To brighter dawns and brighter days.

Each connection, a silent pact,
With healing hands, we face the fact.
Together we rise, spirits blend,
In the grace where hearts can mend.

## Shadows of What Was

In twilight's grasp, the shadows loom,
Memories whisper of fading bloom.
Echoes linger, soft and low,
Remnants of what we used to know.

Through the haze of time, we walk,
In silhouette, we dare to talk.
Each step forward, a ghostly trace,
Haunting smiles on a familiar face.

With every glance, a story told,
Of laughter shared and warmth of old.
Yet in the dark, we seek the light,
Finding strength to face the night.

Shadows dance, they twist and sway,
A bittersweet song of yesterday.
But in the glow of rising sun,
We gather hope, our burdens spun.

From shadows deep, we shall arise,
With open hearts and fearless eyes.
The past shapes us, but it won't confine,
In the light, new paths align.

Milton Keynes UK
Ingram Content Group UK Ltd.
UKHW021630011224
451755UK00010B/543